The YELLOWSTONE KiD

By Johnny Boyd

Illustrated by Jeff Teaford

THE YELLOWSTONE KID

Copyright 2010 © by Johnny Boyd

Author and Publisher Johnny Boyd, contact: ptopress@ptopress.com
Illustrator Jeff Teaford, contact: sooperdooper@comcast.net
Published by PTO Press – Peel the Onion
ISBN: 978-0-9760187-2-8

Cover and Book design by Impressions Design | www.impressionsdesign.net

Thanks to John Carlin, Janice "Rusty" Rust and Genevieve Smith.

Special thanks to Cassia - amorzinha, linda and complete.

Suzie Shane skis! Join her on the hill in *FIRST TRACKS*

TO ORDER BOOKS CONTACT:
ptopress@ptopress.com
www.ptopress.com
Printed in the United States of America

This book is dedicated to the men and women of the National Park Service.
You geyser awesome!

Hi there!

It's Suzie Shane your old pal.

My family and I are going on an adventure to an amazingly beautiful locale.

We'll be traveling to Yellowstone.

Where it is, I don't really know.

My Daddy says there will be animals and trees

and a very active volcano.

I like to bring my friends along;
so you're invited as well.
We'll have so much fun together
and what stories we will tell!

My Mommy and my Daddy
are the people you should meet.
My brother Jay is pretty cool
when he's acting sweet.

Daddy has loaded up the car.

He piled it high with food and drink.

It looks like we're taking everything,

maybe even the kitchen sink!

A road trip in an automobile
can be quite the expedition.
A family vacation in a car
is a great American tradition.

We'll probably drive our car
at least a million miles.
We'll play games and sing songs
that will bring a zillion smiles.

Up ahead I see a gate.
Soon we'll drive into the park.
It's so full of animals;
it looks like Noah's Ark!

We've set up our camping tent
surrounded by lots of trees.
Tonight we will sleep with nature
lulled by the soft, sweet breeze.

I wake up the next morning
and step outside the tent.
The whole world smells like pinecones;
that's such a lovely scent.

Daddy wakes up early to cook some breakfast.

He's now my super-cool-camping-Daddy-dude.

Cooking outside makes meals taste better.

I've never eaten such great food!

A chipmunk begs for scraps,
but from him my food is hidden.
Feeding the animals of Yellowstone
is illegal and forbidden.

If people feed the animals,
they become dependent like a child.
They rely on others for food,
and forget how to be wild.

We leave our camp behind
to go out and take a drive.
Yellowstone is a habitat
where thousands of animals thrive.

The animal that I want to see
can't be found just anywhere.
Yellowstone is the place to see
a great big shaggy bear.

15

I think I see a bear,
but it's just a rocky lump.
Then I see another bear
that turns out to be a stump.

Daddy tells me not to worry;
there is no way to compare.
A lump and a stump are nothing
when you see a real live bear!

We creep up on some animals
and try not to get them stirred.
I attempt to get a photo
of a very large elk herd.

Mommy warns us very quickly:
"That's as close as you can get!
These animals may look tame,
but they certainly are not pets."

Suddenly the elk are jumpy.
They quickly take to their hooves.
The elk start running for their lives,
being chased by hungry wolves.

The elk flee over the horizon
with the pack not far behind.
Perhaps the wolves got dinner
or maybe they were declined.

We stop at a thermal feature.

This one is full of mud.

It bubbles and boils out of the ground

and makes a sound like "grumble-blubber-thud."

Jay races ahead on the boardwalk.

But Daddy stops him on the spot.

"Jay, be careful!" he says.

"You could be cooked like a lobster in a pot!"

19

We visit a grand old hotel
that was built way back when.
It looks just like a work of art,
and it's called the Old Faithful Inn.

The hotel is built near a geyser
that gives the inn its name.
Old Faithful erupts like clockwork;
that's how it earned its fame.

I'm sad I didn't see a bear today
but I keep looking all around.
Daddy takes us to an amphitheater
at the edge of our campground.

A man is speaking there.
His name is Ranger Clark.
He's such an expert on Yellowstone,
I think he owns the park.

"FOR THE BENEFIT AND ENJOYMENT OF THE PEOPLE"

"I do own Yellowstone," he says.
"But you own it, too.
Yellowstone is for everyone
even kids like Jay and you."

Ranger Clark tells tales of fires
that made America frown.
People thought that Yellowstone
would burn down to the ground.

But fire is good for the forest.
It grew back healthier than before!
Fire takes away a little life
but gives back even more.

We drive across the Hayden Valley.
Its plain stretches to the horizon.
It's dotted with beautiful animals,
especially American Bison!

The pioneers called bison buffalo.
Why they did that, I don't know.
It's like calling an eagle a crow.
If I see any pioneers, I'll let them know.

Daddy rents some bikes for all of us
to ride along a trail.

When you see Yellowstone at slower speed
there's so much more detail.

The Grand Canyon of the Yellowstone
is topped by a thundering cascade.
Yellowstone Falls has to be
the most beautiful sight ever made.

"Daddy?" I ask. "Where is the volcano?
I can't see it anywhere."
"You're standing in it," he says.
"It's all around and everywhere."

"A large portion of the park
is inside a huge caldera.
This volcano exploded years ago
in a prehistoric era."

The terraces of Mammoth Hot Springs
are made of calcium carbonate.
I'm not sure what that is,
but I hope it's not something I ate.

On our way back to our camp
I finally see a bear.
He poses for our pictures
and shakes his shaggy hair.

I'm so glad I got to see a bear,
I hope you see one as well.
So when you return from Yellowstone,
you'll have tall tales to tell!

This family vacation in Yellowstone
is the best fun I've ever had.
I love spending time with my brother,
my Mommy and my Dad.

I've had a great time on this vacation,
and I hope you've enjoyed it, too.
The next time I go anywhere
if you can come, please do!

ABOUT THE BOOK

I teamed up with Jeff Teaford in 2004 to create *FIRST TRACKS* and inspire little kids to ski and snowboard. Then I realized that Suzie Shane and her family could do a lot more than ski. She could go to other places and tell kids about them, or remind them of the good times they had when they were on vacation.

Suzie is the ambassador for going outside. I'll grant you that she isn't starring in some grand adventure being chased by bears or dodging other dangers. She is simply recounting what all of us do on a vacation – she sees the sights and returns home safe and sound.

Then the memories begin to slowly fade.

Suzie steps in and becomes that memory in a child's mind. Her story is the experience that shouldn't be forgotten. She keeps the wonder alive that your child felt when that animal crossed your path or that geyser erupted in Yellowstone.

The Yellowstone Kid is Suzie's second grand adventure. Ambassador Shane brings you Yellowstone through a child's eye. And we will never forget.

Johnny Boyd
04/2010